IMAGES
of America

Vons Grocery Company

This Vons logo stood proudly above the Vons corporate offices at 10150 Lower Azusa Road in El Monte, California, for over 30 years until the company's relocation to Arcadia, California, in 1989. (Courtesy of Vons Grocery Company.)

ON THE COVER: Charles Von der Ahe opened Vons store no. 2, one of the first "cash and carry" neighborhood markets, shortly after the turn of the century. This store was located at 6100 Moneta Avenue in Los Angeles. (Courtesy of Jodi Olsen Kelly.)

IMAGES
of America

Vons Grocery Company

Michael L. Stark and Wendy Kennedy

ARCADIA
PUBLISHING

ISBN 978-1-4671-3090-5

Published by Arcadia Publishing
Charleston, South Carolina

Printed in the United States of America

Library of Congress Control Number: 2013942030

For all general information, please contact Arcadia Publishing:
Telephone 843-853-2070
Fax 843-853-0044
E-mail sales@arcadiapublishing.com
For customer service and orders:
Toll-Free 1-888-313-2665

Visit us on the Internet at www.arcadiapublishing.com

This book is dedicated to three important groups of people in Vons history. First, to the founding fathers of Vons who had the vision and ambition to start the company and create a culture that would survive for generations. Second, to the senior leaders of Vons who, over the years, provided continuous guidance and vision to grow the company into a successful, premier organization. Finally, to the thousands of dedicated Vons employees who proudly served their customers and significantly contributed to the success of Vons Grocery Company.

Contents

Foreword

This is truly a "story that needed to be told"—a story about a remarkable company that started with one market in the heart of Los Angeles led by an intuitive and moral family that grew into a billion-dollar supermarket empire in Southern California, creating thousands of careers and serving millions of customers. I'm pleased to add my comments to the many contributors, especially Mike Stark and Wendy Kennedy, who worked diligently to organize and create this memorable book.

The founding Von der Ahe family built the company on principles of honesty, the importance of families, and a culture of respect that made us all proud to be members of the Vons team. I can remember when I joined, Charles, Ted, Wil, and Walter Von der Ahe all made their own significant contributions as to how the company operated and resulted in the unique culture that became the fabric of Vons. This culture was so embedded that, remarkably, well after the Von der Ahe family was no longer involved in the business, the "spirit of Vons" culture remained.

Credit for this continuing culture must also go to those who followed the Von der Ahes—leaders who worked diligently to ensure that the company remained a "special place to work"—veteran employees like Ken Olsen, Jerry Fahey, Bill Davila, and Roger Stangeland.

The Vons experience taught us to listen to and learn from employees, customers, and our communities as well as to respect our competitors. This knowledge led to Vons becoming an extremely innovative and successful merchant. Countless supermarket innovations, from merchandising to advertising, came from this culture. We were proud to work at Vons.

We were also very proud that Vons, its competitors, and the industry were deeply involved in local communities and charities. While the term "corporate citizen" was yet to be coined, the industry—and Vons in particular—led the way.

I was fortunate to have started my career at Vons. As I look back, the lessons I learned there were the foundation for any success I achieved in my business career. As it also turned out, the Vons experience served me well in other facets of my life, as I believe it did for many others. From my first day in the advertising department in 1958 to my last day in 1997, I was always grateful for my Vons roots and the lessons I learned.

As I said earlier, this is truly a story that needed to be told—a story of great success and a source of pride for all of us who were part of this remarkable journey.

—Lawrence A. Del Santo, November 2013
President of Vons Grocery Company, 1973–1975
Chairman and President of Vons Grocery Company, 1994–1997

Lawrence (Larry) A. Del Santo began and ended his career with Vons. He joined the company in 1958 after serving in the military. His first position was in the advertising department, and he quickly rose to the position of president. In 1983, he left City Products (which then owned Vons), to become president of Lucky Stores, which was subsequently purchased by American Stores Company Inc. In 1994, Del Santo returned to Vons as chairman and chief executive officer before retiring in 1997 after Vons was acquired by Safeway. He has served on various boards, including those of SuperValu and PetSmart. He also served as a trustee of the University of San Francisco. He is married and has 12 children and 35 grandchildren. (Courtesy of Larry Del Santo.)

Acknowledgments

The idea for this book came from retired Vons president Jerry Fahey. In September 2011, at a Vons reunion, Fahey was addressing the audience and said, "I sure wish someone would write a book about this great company!" The authors looked at each other and said, in unison, "We can do that!"

We would like to acknowledge the following people:

Tom Von der Ahe for so graciously allowing us access to a library of documents from the estate of his father, Wil Von der Ahe. There was truly a treasure trove of documents, with some dating back to the 1920s.

Ken Olsen for sharing documents and, more importantly, his vivid memories of the company he still loves and is so proud to have led.

Jerry Fahey for providing the inspiration to write the book and a timeline for the many significant events that occurred over 75 years.

Dorothy Davila for many boxes of documents and memorabilia that added to the rich pictorial history depicted in the following pages.

Pete Horn III, Bud Moorman, and Audrey Burkett Nelson for sharing their personal Vons collectibles that added important detail.

Mitch and Susan Crawford for providing many photographs and stories of Vons people enjoying camaraderie over the past 30 years.

Jodi Olsen Kelly, EdD, for saving all those early editions of the Vons internal newsletter, *Crax'N'Fax*, and sharing them with us.

Sharon Gresswell for sharing some of the personal effects that C.R. "Dick" Gresswell, her spouse, kept over his almost 50 years at Vons.

Unless otherwise noted, all photographs except those in Chapter Seven are from Vons Grocery Company publications. The photographs in Chapter Seven are from Jon Edwards, of Jon Edwards Photography, who graciously photographed the first Vons management reunion in 2009 and has allowed us to use the photographs in this book.

INTRODUCTION

Vons Grocery Company was built on a foundation of three basic principles: care for the customer, care for employees, and care for the community. This philosophy illustrates "the spirit of Vons" that started with the founders in 1906 and has continued for over 100 years.

Looking back over the company's long history, it is easy to see why Vons has been a leader in the industry. Vons has not only provided for consumers' basic needs but has delighted them with innovative service offerings and quality products. Vons has maintained a "growth mindset" by constructing new stores, acquiring other reputable grocery chains, expanding into other regions and communities, and operating other store formats. By changing, adapting, and evolving over time, Vons has remained on the leading edge. This only occurred by continually looking ahead, as the founding family did.

Vons has been a model in the supermarket industry—a company that has gone through many changes and challenges and come out on top. Through these evolutions, one thing has remained the same: the hard work and dedication of the people of Vons. As Bill Davila, president emeritus, said in the Vons internal newsletter, *Crax'N'Fax*, in 1996, "At Vons, the workforce has always been like a family. There's always been closeness and a sense of teamwork throughout the company. That atmosphere has always brought out the best in everyone."

Vons has continually invested in its employees by providing training and development programs at all levels. The company has been a major supporter of the Food Industry Management Program at the University of Southern California.

Through the years, the Vons family has not only cared for customers and employees but also for those in the communities they serve. Vons has been a strong corporate citizen, "giving back" and supporting such organizations as the City of Hope and school programs such as "Apples for the Students," which provides computers to schools. Vons has also been a strong supporter of many different food banks and other local causes.

In 1984, Vons was designated as the official supermarket of the Los Angeles Olympics. In the Vons internal newsletter, *Crax'N'Fax*, Ken Olsen, Vons' retired president, commented, "they said they had researched the major food chains and felt Vons was best equipped to be the major food supplier." In a deal worked out with the International Olympic Committee, the Company agreed to provide food for more than 12,000 athletes, coaches, and trainers in the Olympic Village. "We look at this as an investment in the community," explained Jerry Fahey, Vons' president in 1984. Food worth $8 million was provided to the committee at cost for preparation by an independent food service organization. The balance, worth $2 million, was donated by Vons.

As you read through the pages of this book, it is our hope that you find a rich history of a truly great company. It was our honor to work for Vons for many years and our pleasure to write this book.

This artist's rendition of a photograph of Vons store no. 2 was used to celebrate the company's 69th anniversary.

One

Early Years
1900s–1920s

Vons Grocery Company began in 1906 as a small market on the corner of Seventh and Figueroa Streets in Los Angeles. Over the years, Vons grew to become the leading supermarket chain in Southern California. Today, Vons has more than 300 supermarkets that cover an area ranging from Las Vegas, Nevada, to the Pacific Ocean and from Fresno to the Mexican border.

Charles Von der Ahe, the founder of Vons Grocery Company, started his career in the grocery business by working as a delivery boy in Illinois. He worked for a number of markets while transitioning out west to take up residence in Southern California. Once there, he opened his first market with a total investment of $1,200 and a philosophy of putting the customer first.

Von der Ahe was recognized as an innovator in the grocery industry. He created the "cash and carry" concept, which replaced the "charge and deliver" methodology that was rapidly disappearing. He also brought in fresh meat and produce by leasing out areas in his stores to local vendors and neighborhood butchers, so shoppers no longer had to travel all over town to check off all the items on their grocery lists. Von der Ahe expanded the number of his "grocertarias" to 87 stores in 1929.

Anticipating the looming financial crisis, in 1928 Von der Ahe sold his markets to the McMarr Stores, which were eventually purchased by Safeway. Soon afterward, Von der Ahe retired. However, what began as an early retirement turned out to be only a short vacation from the business he loved. The Von der Ahe family was back in the grocery business just three years later as Charles financed the efforts of his two sons, Ted and Wil.

Emil (left) and Charles Von der Ahe are pictured here inside the original Vons store no. 1 at Seventh and Figueroa Streets in Los Angeles. Two years later, this site was demolished, and Vons was relocated to 48th Street and Vermont Avenue. The original site was converted to the Barker Brothers furniture warehouse, which was later used as a filming location for many Hollywood movies.

In the early 1900s, many markets were designed with open storefronts. Vons store no. 1, originally opened in 1906 by Charles Von der Ahe, was relocated two years later to this storefront at 48th Street and Vermont Avenue in Los Angeles. Emil Von der Ahe, Charles's brother, is standing in front of the store.

Standing in front of Vons store no. 3 is Al Schenck (left), the butcher at this store. His grandson Gary later became a store manager for Vons. The men on the right are unidentified.

In 1926, Vons celebrated by promoting its annual $1 Sale.

Vons started moving its inventory between stores with its own trucks by 1925. This was one of Vons' first trucks.

Vons started baking their own products and sold Vons branded bread at this store located at 44th and Hoover Streets in Los Angeles. The year of this photograph was 1926. Emil Von der Ahe is at far right; the other three people are unidentified.

This is the second Vons store, which was located at 6100 Moneta Avenue in Los Angeles. By May 1920, there were nine Vons stores operating in downtown Los Angeles, with two additional stores planned for opening by the end of the year.

Ed Reynolds, who was still running Vons store no. 6 in 1948, is pictured here behind the checkstand of Vons store no. 15 in 1927.

Charles Von der Ahe started his business on a philosophy of always providing great customer service, as portrayed in this photograph from 1926 that shows the checker focusing her full attention on the customer.

By 1925, Vons needed its own fleet of trucks to service the company's 87 stores located throughout the greater Los Angeles region.

Two

Pioneering Years 1930s–1950s

Ted and Wil Von der Ahe opened Vons store no. 1 in Lynwood with a $2,500 investment from their father, Charles. The brothers numbered the second round of Vons stores starting with no. 1, even though the first round of Vons stores started in 1906 by their father also started with no. 1. By 1934, the chain had grown to three retail grocery stores run with innovation and a new style of customer service. In the third store, the brothers decided to own and operate their own meat and produce departments instead of leasing them to outside vendors. This allowed them to be more in control of service, quality, and establishing fair prices that shoppers had come to expect from Vons.

By the start of World War II, the company operated 12 stores and had over 300 employees. Vons reached milestones when the first postwar market opened in 1947, followed by the well-publicized grand opening of Vons' new flagship store no. 15—located in Los Angeles at the intersection of Santa Barbara Avenue and Crenshaw Boulevard—on February 3, 1948. This 50,300-square-foot market united all of the innovative concepts that the Von der Ahes and other grocers had been experimenting with for years. Not only was this a big day for the shoppers of Los Angeles, it also established Vons as a leader in the grocery industry and the Von der Ahe family as innovators in the retail food industry.

The store featured self-service departments such as meat, produce, and a delicatessen; a large meat-refrigeration room; a check-cashing booth; and a communication system throughout the store. Vons' administrative offices were also located in the mezzanine area of the store.

The opening of store no. 15 brought Vons to a new level and enabled the company to obtain new financing and new sites for future growth.

In 1958, Vons became a public corporation and was listed on the New York Stock Exchange. At that time, the company operated 28 stores, each measuring around 25,000 square feet, and was annually grossing approximately $100 million.

Vons store no. 1 was an open-front market and the beginning of the Vons chain as it is known today. Opened in 1932, this market run by Ted, Wil, and Charles Von der Ahe became the nucleus of a chain that would grow into a dominant supermarket company.

Vons store no. 8, located at Irolo and Eighth Streets, opened on January 6, 1936. Free parking, an early innovation of the Von der Ahes, was still featured in advertisements. This location still serves as an inner-city market operated by JONS International Marketplace.

Van de Kamp Bakery was featured in special areas inside supermarkets in the 1930s and 1940s. This Van de Kamp bakery was inside Vons store no. 8 in the late 1930s.

This c. 1939 image shows Vons store no. 8. Open-front stores were still popular at this time. Note the liquor department at left.

The grand opening of Vons store no. 2 was held in 1939. This was one of the chain's top-grossing stores for many years. It was later remodeled before being completely rebuilt in 1948.

This c. 1938 photograph of the Service Deli in Vons store no. 11 demonstrates the service deli concept that was so popular before World War II. The deli was staffed with five clerks on hand to sell everything from chow mein to Tillamook cheese (then priced at 20¢ per pound). Wieners, bologna, and salami were on sale for 17¢ per pound, while boiled ham was 17¢ per half-pound.

Vons store no. 4, located at 8106 Beverly Boulevard in Los Angeles, opened in 1933 and soon became the busiest little market in Los Angeles. Bargains—such as C&H Sugar on sale for 19¢ per five-pound bag—helped to build sales.

This 1947 image shows the construction of Vons store no. 15 at the corner of Santa Barbara Avenue and Crenshaw Boulevard in Los Angeles. Note the wide-open, undeveloped area looking south of the location toward Windsor Hills.

This image shows Vons store no. 15 just before its grand opening on January 27, 1948. The *Christian Science Monitor* heralded the store as a "super-duper market" when it opened, and with just cause. It occupied a choice spot in a planned integrated cluster of new stores—two department stores and a dozen other businesses—all grouped around a 7,200-car parking lot. It attracted shoppers from miles away, proving that the combination of available parking and centralized stores was a postwar trend that was impossible to beat.

Vons store no. 15 contained a mural that spanned the wall behind the produce department. The store also contained a service meat and fish department, a check-cashing booth, a snack bar, a lounge, a powder room, and restrooms.

In the old days at Vons store no. 2 in Santa Monica, nine butchers were on hand to assist customers at the service meat counter.

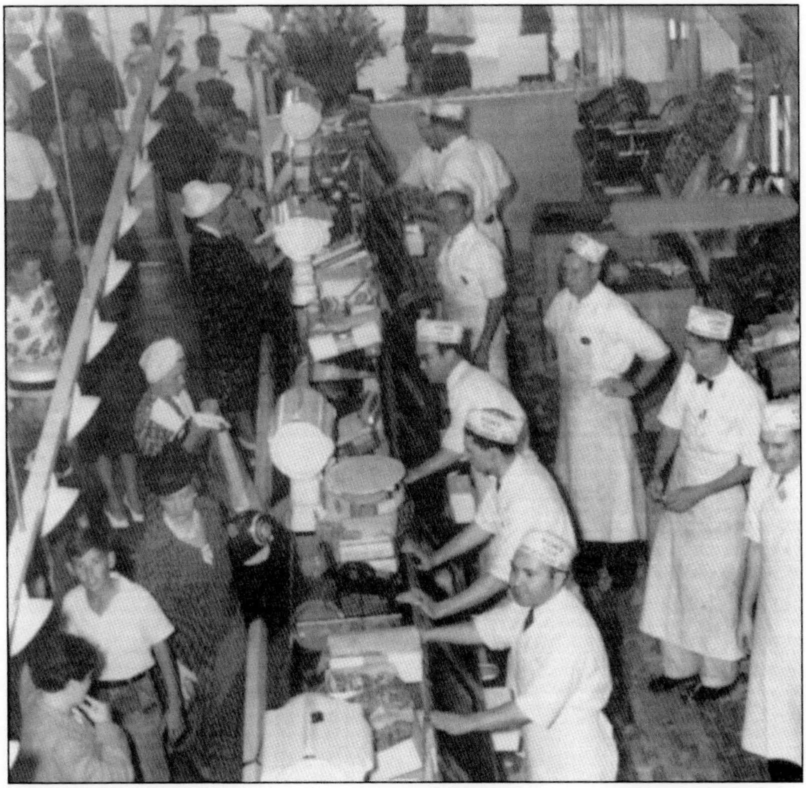

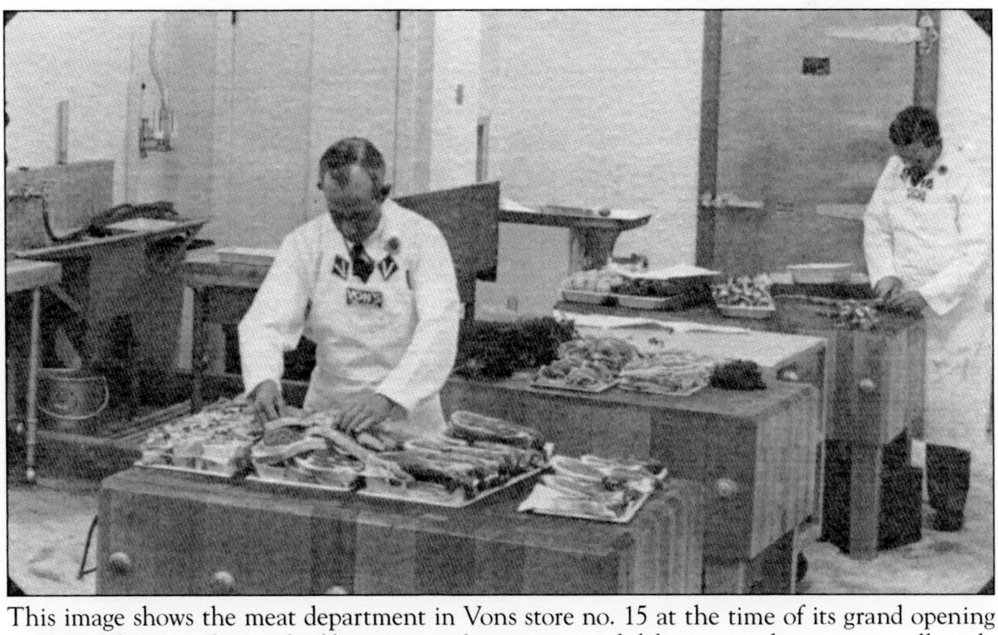

This image shows the meat department in Vons store no. 15 at the time of its grand opening in 1948. The store featured self-service produce, meat, and delicatessen departments, all made possible by the innovation of prepackaged perishables.

Future Vons president Ken Olsen (right) started his career in 1949 as a meat cutter at Vons store no. 9, later transferring to Vons store no. 15, as meat department manager.

This c. 1950 photograph shows the snack bar at Vons store no. 15.

This early Vons was located in south Los Angeles in the late 1940s. Note the open-air produce stand containing self-service scales and offering pears for 15¢ per pound, avocados for 19¢ per pound, bananas for 18¢ per pound, and 5 pounds of oranges for 29¢.

This is the Santee Produce Warehouse, which served all the Vons markets in the late 1940s.

The Los Angeles County Sheriff's Department sponsored a training course for security agents of the retail food industry. This three-day course focused on shoplifting, pilfering, and fraudulent checks. Los Angeles County sheriff Peter Pitchess commented, "One Southern California grocery chain reported bad checks that year cost them $75,000, and there were 800 cases of shoplifting." Pictured here are, from left to right, L. Rudy Weber, Vons security manager; Wil Von der Ahe; Harry Elliot, Vons security; Los Angeles County sheriff Peter J. Pitchess; and Don Lundquist, Vons security.

Ken Hansen is shown unloading grocery items that have been delivered to the distribution center for later delivery to the stores.

On Friday, November 16, 1956, Vons Distribution Center was featured on the live broadcast of *Success Story*, a locally-aired television show on Channel 11 KTTV. The broadcast covered various aspects of the distribution center, including the grocery warehouse, the produce warehouse, and the deli kitchen. The program featured interviews with Don Bushmeyer, Vons distribution manager, and Wil Von der Ahe. The emcee of the show, Ken Peters, is riding the Towveyer cart at far right. (Courtesy of the estate of Wil Von der Ahe.)

This photograph of the *Success Story* broadcast shows the deli kitchen. The employees are unidentified, emcee Ken Peters is holding a microphone at center, and Ed Hirschman, deli kitchen manager, is at right with his back to the camera. (Courtesy of the estate of Wil Von der Ahe.)

At a Southern California food industry event, Bob and Dolores Hope (center) speak with Linda (far left) and Charles Von der Ahe, Vons chairman and founder. Linda and Charles were heavily involved in the grocery industry and the community, continually making philanthropic donations to a variety of charitable organizations. (Courtesy of the estate of Wil Von der Ahe.)

This image shows a worker in the Vons deli kitchen using a "state-of-the-art" automated machine to fill empty cartons with salad for sale in deli sections at Vons stores.

This is one of the many grand openings of a new Vons store. Among those pictured are: Charles and Linda Von der Ahe (immediately left of the front door), Wil and Mary Jane Von der Ahe, and Ted and Dorothy Von der Ahe.

This c. 1955 photograph shows a young Bill Davila (future president of Vons) when he was a produce clerk in Los Angeles.

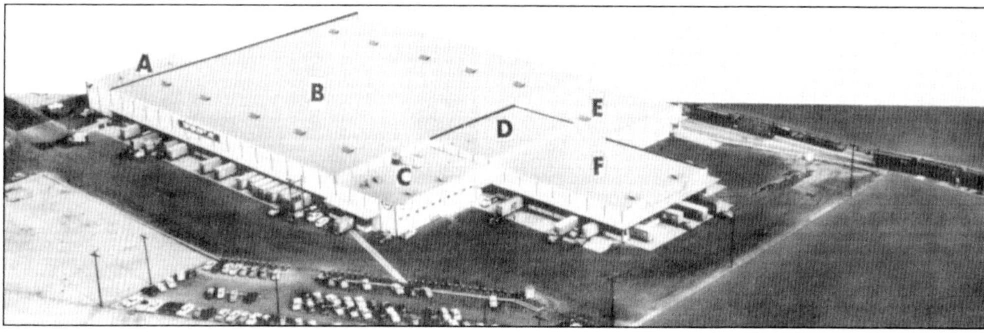

This is an aerial view of the "mammoth" Vons Distribution Center located at 2700 S. Garfield Avenue in Los Angeles. The structure spanned 216,000 square feet and included 54 steel roll-up doors and 33-foot-high walls. It was opened in August 1956. The letters on the image correspond to the following areas: A) sign shop, B) grocery warehouse, C) delicatessen kitchen, D) produce offices, E) produce warehouse, F) produce receiving docks.

This was the ground-breaking ceremony for the Vons executive office building on Santa Barbara Boulevard, near the Crenshaw central shopping district, constructed to house the administrative personnel. The new offices were to occupy 23,000 square feet. Attending the ceremony are, from left to right, J. Edward Martin, representing Albert G. Martin & Associates architects and engineers; Walter Von der Ahe; Wil Von der Ahe; Ted Von der Ahe; Charles Von Der Ahe; Lawrence McNeil, head of McNeil Construction Company; and Bruce McNeil (Lawrence's son).

The role of the front-end man was vital to an efficient store operation. The front-end man kept close watch over the checkstands to ensure that they were performing properly, as well as approving checks and maintaining customer relations. In this image, Ed Chamberlin is pictured approving a check.

The last contact with the customer was the box boy, later referred to as the clerk's helper (and, more recently, as the courtesy clerk). Before their first day on the job, these employees all received training on how to properly load groceries and take care of customers. Other important areas of focus included courtesy and grooming to insure outstanding appearance.

Don Bushmeyer, distribution center manager (right), and Dick Cressey, dispatcher, are pictured planning Vons truck routes. Cressey was responsible for all trucks that left the distribution center.

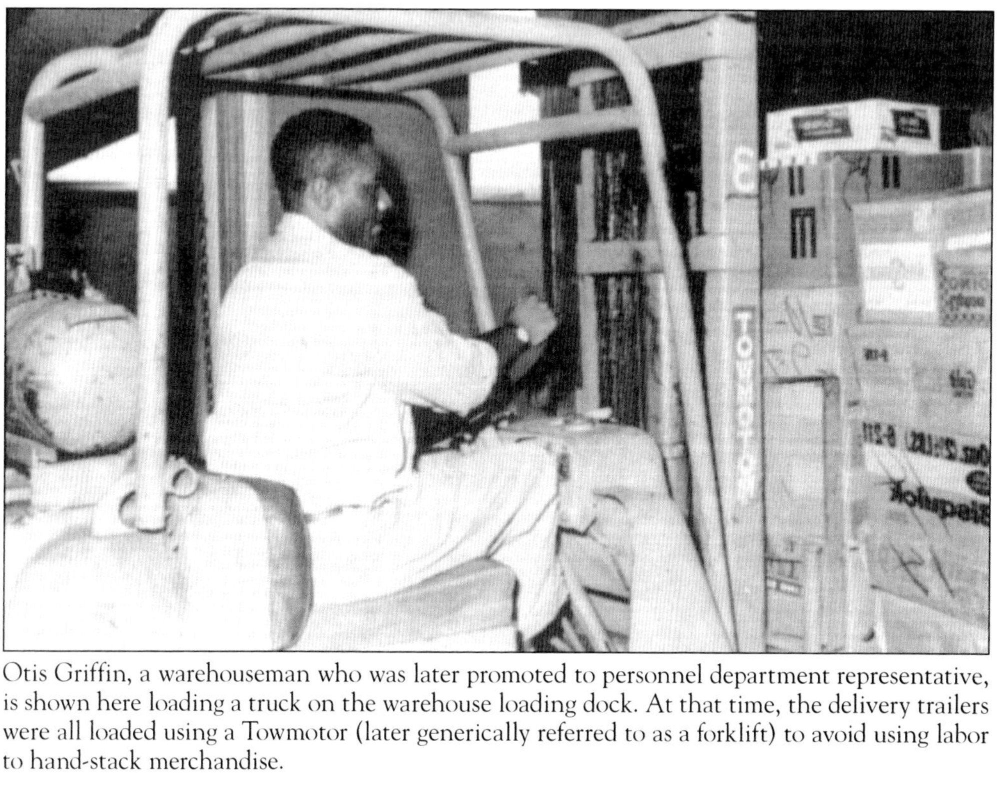

Otis Griffin, a warehouseman who was later promoted to personnel department representative, is shown here loading a truck on the warehouse loading dock. At that time, the delivery trailers were all loaded using a Towmotor (later generically referred to as a forklift) to avoid using labor to hand-stack merchandise.

Three

Growth Years
1960s–1970s

In 1960, Vons merged with Shopping Bag Food Stores. Shopping Bag had been operating in Southern California for approximately 30 years and operated 38 markets. The new organization had 66 markets doing business under the Vons and Shopping Bag brand. Particular emphasis was placed on understanding local markets and arranging space accordingly, a practice that has continued up to the present day. Seven years later, the Federal Trade Commission challenged the merger, and after two lower court victories, the US Supreme Court reversed the decisions and ordered an immediate divestiture.

In a *Crax'N'Fax* article, Ted Von der Ahe commented at that time that "it is with regret and remorse that we lose the Shopping Bag stores. I don't think the decision was correct but, nevertheless, it was a decision by the highest court in the land and we have to comply with it."

In 1969, Vons was purchased by Household Finance Corporation and operated under the Household Merchandising division of Household International. At that time, the chain consisted of 80 stores and had 5,700 employees. Household acquired Vons in a stock exchange deal estimated to be worth $120 million.

The 1970s were a period of explosive growth and innovation for Vons, starting with the company's movement into the San Diego area and acquisition of DeFalco Supermarkets. Through construction and acquisition, Vons grew to 161 stores ranging from Bakersfield to the Mexican border. During this decade, Vons found a new outlet for its own products by selling them wholesale to retailers and fast-food restaurants.

Looking for new ways to energize its customers, Vons opened the first Value Center in 1973 with a service bakery, fish counter, and pharmacy. The store had expanded general merchandise and health-and-beauty sections and offered shoppers a one-stop shopping experience. This "combo" concept later developed into the Pavilions stores in 1987.

Vons also opened a new meat service center in 1977, processing hanging beef for their stores and producing hamburger patties for fast-food restaurants. This allowed Vons to better control the quality of their meat and allowed meat cutters in the stores to focus on customer service. The Meat Service Center also contained the Vons quality assurance laboratory, which tested every shipment of Vons' private-label products to guarantee high quality.

Automation also came to the stores in the 1970s. UPC scanners were first introduced to Vons at the Granada Hills store in 1978.

The 1960s began with Charles Von der Ahe (seated) in the role of chairman and his son Ted in the role of president and chief executive officer. This was the beginning of a period of tremendous expansion, starting with the Vons merger with Shopping Bag Food Stores in March 1960.

Linda and Charles Von der Ahe, chairman of the board and founder of Vons, prepare to cut into a beautiful cake created by the bakery department in celebration of Vons 100th store.

Following the merger with Shopping Bag, Vons immediately rebranded their distribution trailers to improve brand recognition. Ted Von der Ahe is pictured here with a newly rebranded trailer.

Every year, Vons hosted a 4-U Fund holiday party at the Palladium in Hollywood. The tickets were $5 each, and the proceeds were used to assist employees in need. This is an undated photograph from one of the 4-U Fund holiday parties.

This photograph shows Vons store no. 2 in Santa Monica shortly after its grand reopening on November 2, 1966.

In this image, Wil Von der Ahe (left), executive vice president, reminds Don Hays, store manager, what old Vons store no. 2 looked like when it opened in 1939. The store was remodeled several times in the 1940s and 1950s and was completely demolished and rebuilt in 1966 so that the new, two-level store could better serve the people of Santa Monica.

This image shows Wil Von der Ahe, executive vice president, and W.A. Christensen, general manager, being interviewed on live television by KTLA News at the time of the grand reopening of Vons store no. 2 in 1966.

Pictured here is an unidentified checker at Vons store no. 2 shortly after the store's grand reopening. Note the Blue Chip Stamp dial dispenser located to the left of the cash register. At the time, Blue Chip Stamps were offered at all Vons stores as one of many ways for the company to remain competitive. Many retailers offered the stamps to retain customers, as the stamps could be redeemed for merchandise at Blue Chip Stamp stores.

Ted and Dorothy Von der Ahe were extremely generous, making significant donations to a variety of charitable organizations. In this picture, Ted (third from left) is pictured with John Wayne (far left) and Dorothy (far right) at the Our Little Brothers and Sisters Orphanage and School in Cuernavaca, Mexico. Ted and Dorothy frequently visited this orphanage to provide financial and emotional support. (Courtesy of the estate of Wil Von der Ahe.)

In the late 1960s, Vons made a significant investment in the environment by converting its truck fleet to use propane fuel. Until that time, the Vons fleet was powered by diesel fuel.

The Vons and Shopping Bag markets contained over 15,000 items, many of which were highly perishable. The orderly delivery of these items required deploying 269 trucks from the El Monte Distribution Center every day to service all stores.

These members of Vons' personnel department are pictured at the 1967 Annual Checker of the Year brunch in Los Angeles. Pictured here are, from left to right, (first row) Virginia Rizatto, Mary McClenahan, Midge Young, Faye Haas, Pat Maloney, and Julie Siemek; (second row) Bill Heinen, Ken Doyle, Bob Whitaker, Joe Cirallo, and Wilma Yorkovich.

In this photograph, a member of the Vons bakery production team is inspecting fresh bakery goods for distribution to the stores. Vons bakery was located in the El Monte distribution center.

Vons deli kitchen was highly recognized for the fresh deli salads and cheeses it produced for distribution to the stores. Pictured here, deli kitchen manager Bill Madison was recognized in the industry as one of the top producers of retail-ready deli products. He began his career at Vons store no. 8 in the early 1940s. After spending five years in the Pacific in World War II, he returned to Vons to continue his career. Bill met his wife, Lorraine, when she was a deli clerk at Vons store no. 11.

The courtesy booth provided a central place where most customer service needs could be addressed. The booth was usually located between the checkstands in the middle front of the store. In this photograph, Pauline is waiting to greet her next customer. Note the picture of future vice president Jim McLaughlin when he was a young store manager.

The design and layout of the weekly Vons advertisement was something that took time and imagination to ensure it was attractive and inviting to the customer. Pictured here creating the layout of a weekly newspaper advertisement are, from left to right, Bill Davila, Jerry Fahey, unidentified, and Mike Sresovich.

In the early 1970s, Vons was recognized for its contribution to cleaning the air of Los Angeles with its investment in a propane-powered fleet of trucks. Pictured here are Los Angeles mayor Sam Yorty (left), Wil Von der Ahe (center), and Ken Olsen. (Courtesy of the estate of Wil Von der Ahe.)

This photograph shows Vons executive management team working on store operations planning. Pictured are, from left to right, Don Stuetz, Jerry Fahey, Mike Sresovich, and Ken Olsen.

Vons was committed to the ongoing development of the management team to insure excellent service and execution. Twice each year, a management training class was hosted and organized by Vons' training department. The goal was to prepare employees selected by district managers to learn more about Vons' business and to prepare them to be leaders. The class focused on leadership skills, financial skills, and enhancing the participants' knowledge of the company and the food industry. The training was impactful because classes were conducted by senior leaders and executives from all areas of the company. All-day classes were held once a week for 10 weeks. This photograph shows the members of the fall 1972 class. Pictured are, from left to right, (first row) Jerry Rican, Wally Barnett, Don Admire, Bob Jamison, Dennis Schmidt, John Harding, Ken Griffin, and Bill Kendig; (second row) Merle McNinch, Jim Buetow, Barry Kidd, Vince Gallegos, Ed Marrujo, Bob DeLorto, Stan Linowski, and Ed Grieco; (third row) Larry Larson, Check Zepf, Scuffie Shigg, Ben Skinner, Rich Peterson, John Alexander, Duane Hale, and Gary Finnegan.

Vons' commitment to the community included an annual American Red Cross blood drive at all of its stores and the corporate office. This photograph shows members of Vons store no. 57 who donated to the company's annual blood drive in July 1974. Pictured are, from left to right, store manager Phil Mooney, Steve Lawson, Mary Jancic, Vern Cantrell (kneeling), John Salazar, Edna Reed, Nat Anderson, Nadine Brown, and Keith James.

As supermarket POS (point of sale) technology was advancing, Vons explored new checkstand scanners to remain competitive and improve productivity. On March 18, 1974, a delegation of Vons management visited IBM and received a demonstration of their new scanner, the IBM 3660; pictured here are, from left to right, Barney Sheridan, Don Stuetz, Larry Del Santo, Mike Sresovich, Wil Von der Ahe, Elmer Larsen, an unidentified IBM representative, and Bob Hearn. (Courtesy of the estate of Wil Von der Ahe.)

Members of the main office staff are shows during one of the annual holiday luncheons. Pictured here are, from left to right, (first row) Mary Thompson, Linda Schlinger, and unidentified; (second row) Sandy Weir, Glen Johnson, Barney Sheridan, Bob Schiffmacher, and Audrey Burkett Nelson.

Each year, Vons hosted an Annual Service Awards dinner at the Century Plaza Hotel to recognize employees with 10, 15, or more years of service to the company. Special recognition was given to those with 25-, 30-, and 35-year anniversaries. Longtime employee Sam Johnson is pictured with his wife at the 1974 Annual Service Awards dinner.

Here, Mary Jane Herron is being presented with a gold watch for reaching her 25th anniversary in 1974 with Vons. Herron is pictured with Ken Doyle (left), vice president of personnel and labor relations, and Ken Olsen (right), executive vice president.

Sam Helbley was installed into the "Oldies but Goodies Club" for reaching his 35th anniversary with Vons in 1974. Helbley is pictured with Larry Del Santo (left), president, and Ken Olsen (right), executive vice president.

In 1974, Vons opened a new store format in Rancho Bernardo. Vons store no. 79 was billed as "15 Stores in One" because it contained a butcher shop, a bakery, a fish market, an old-world deli, and a number of other departments not usually found in a grocery store. The opening of this store generated a lot of excitement in the Rancho Bernardo community and in the retail grocery industry. This is a view of the activity at the front of the store on the morning of the grand opening.

During the 1974 grand opening of the Rancho Bernardo Vons store no. 79, Dick London, vice president of new store formats, displayed his talent and merchandising abilities.

Kathleen Newman prepares freshly baked whole-wheat bread (costing 55¢ per loaf) in the hot bakery at Vons store no. 79.

Members of the 1975 Vons management training class included, from left to right, (first row) Ron Humphrey, Bob Wright, Jeannette Beetschen, Paula Gamble, Helen Smith, Gerry Dunn, Sonny Schrey, and Gary Miller; (second row), Ralph Ryan, Howard Washington, Bob Clark, Dick Spezzano, Mel Brown, John Morgan, Vern Morrow, and Rich Franceshini.

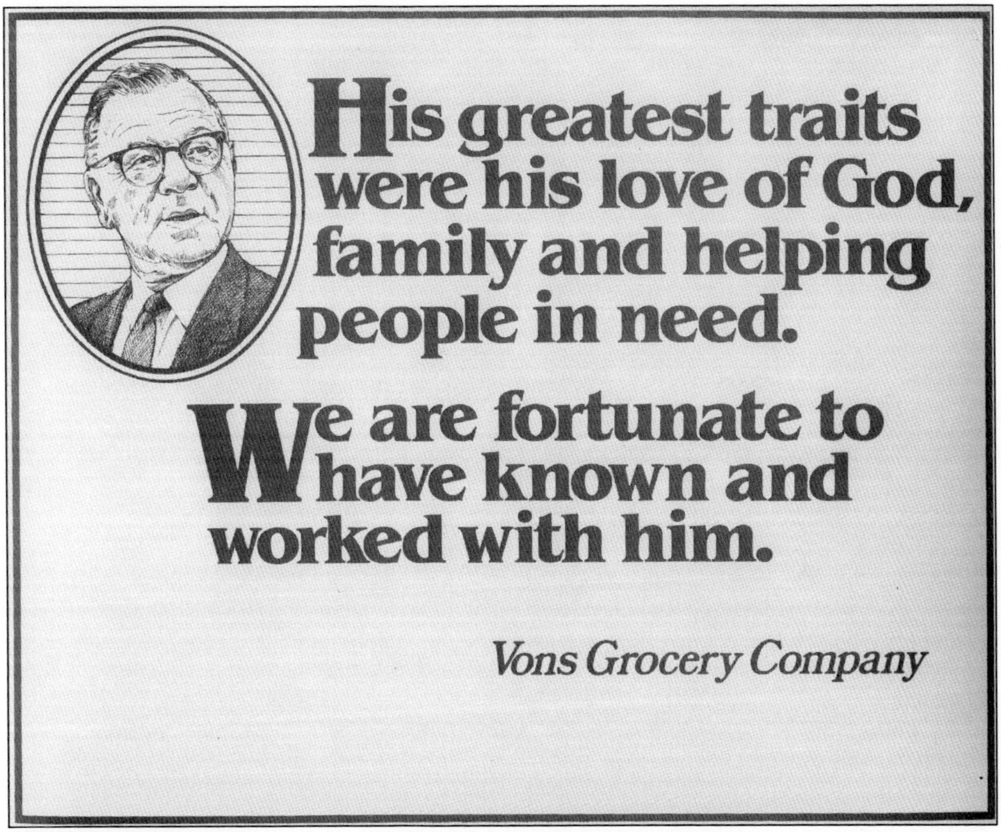

This tribute to Ted Von der Ahe, former Vons president, was printed in *Crax'N'Fax* upon his passing in 1978.

The Universal Product Code (UPC) was implemented in the early 1970s with the goal that 80 percent of all retail food products would be converted by 1976. The UPC was a common denominator for an entire industry that signified the will of the grocery industry to standardize. The zero at left indicates that the item is one regularly retailed in grocery stores. The next five digits indicate it is a product of the specific manufacturer. The last five digits indicate what the item is and its size. The computer was programmed to read this UPC when it was passed over the scanner by a checker and assign a price to the item.

The supermarket industry partnered with the University of Southern California to create a program focusing on food marketing management. Each year, Vons would select a limited number of employees viewed as high achievers to attend this program. Pictured here are members of the 1977 class. They are, from left to right, (first row) Kris Robinson (from Vons store no. 26) and Bob Brady (from the Hawaiian Gardens store); (second row) Gary Hammett (from Vons store no. 74), Wendy Hodkinson (Kennedy) (from Vons store no. 83), and Chris Brown (from Vons store no. 111).

Celebrating at the annual holiday party, from left to right are Jim Dunbar, director of employment; Faye Haas, director of consumer affairs; and Ken Doyle, vice president of personnel and labor relations.

In 1974, the Vons fleet took first place at the Los Angeles Safety Council annual dinner. Pictured outside of the truck, from left to right, are N.C. Fontenot, Joe Uribe, Farrow Yano, and Tony Anaya. The driver in the cab is unidentified.

Vons hosted an annual Checkers' Brunch to recognize the top checkers from each store and district, and one checker was selected as Checker of the Year. This image shows the district winners and the Checker of the Year for 1976.

At the 1976 Checkers' Brunch, some of the instructors dressed in patriotic costumes to honor the nation's bicentennial. Pictured here are, from left to right, Wilma Yorkovich, May Nakano, Virginia Acierni, Pat Maloney, Julie Siemek, and Janet Reedy.

In the 1970s, Vons made a significant investment in technology to meet various business needs ranging from labor scheduling and order management to financial reporting and payroll. Ron Smallwood is pictured here monitoring the IBM mainframe computer located in the first floor of the Vons main office.

Pat Heflin is pictured here entering data into a data terminal connected to the IBM mainframe computer.

C.R. "Dick" Gresswell was promoted to manage the Vons security department in 1974. Under Gresswell's leadership, the security department, later known as the loss prevention department, was one of the leading retail loss prevention departments in California. Gresswell retired in 2004 after working for almost 50 years at Vons. Like many Vons employees, he began his career as a clerk's helper in a Vons store.

Members of the 1977 management training class are, from left to right, (first row) Dick Baker, Chuck Lamont, Al Andersen, Phil Turner, Jeannine Ross, Randy Hendrickson, Dan Granger, Ron Fujishige, and Juan Jaime; (second row) Joe Wahlrab, Bob Andersen, Bob Dyer, Pat Shelton, Dan Lionello, Jim McDaniel, Gary Durden, Paul Heller, Gary Posey, and Bob Rorex; (third row) Ray Carabajal, Paul Szilagi, Dennis Garon, John Turley, Andreas Kompier, Ken Montague, and Richard Stockard.

In the mid-1970s, Vons opened a meat service center within their distribution center in El Monte. The meat service center received railcars full of hanging beef that were processed and prepared for retail. The processes employed at the plant resulted in less than two percent waste, as every part of the steer was used in the process, and bones were sent to a rendering company for further use. This image shows the production line cutting beef in preparation for delivery to Vons stores.

Four

Expansion Years 1980s

In the early 1980s, Vons expanded north into the Fresno area by opening five stores—two of them on the same day! In this time period, the company began to emphasize the importance of combining coupon promotions with in-store product demonstrations to entice more conservative shoppers to try new foods.

In 1984, Vons scored a tremendous coup when the company was designated as the official supermarket of the Los Angeles Summer Olympics. Under a deal negotiated with the International Olympic Committee, Vons agreed to provide food for more than 12,000 athletes, coaches, and trainers in the Olympic Village. Food worth $8 million was provided to the committee at cost for preparation by an independent foodservice organization. The balance, worth $2 million, was donated by Vons. In return, Vons was guaranteed a number of exclusive merchandising and advertising opportunities. This milestone event brought incredible recognition to Vons.

Also in 1984, Roger E. Stangeland, a Household executive and chairman of Vons, created a plan to purchase the Household Merchandising division of Household International in a management-led buyout. The deal, valued at approximately $750 million, was the largest retail leveraged buyout in the United States at the time and was completed in January 1986.

In 1985, Vons opened the first Pavilions store in Garden Grove, a 75,000-square-foot combination store under the direction of a Vons management team that traveled throughout the country studying best-in-class supermarket operations. Pavilions offered huge food and non-food sections and was viewed as a model for future combination stores. The Pavilions superstore concept was an immediate success and set new sales records for Vons.

In 1986, Vons acquired the 10-store Pantry Supermarkets chain that was operating in Orange County. Pantry Supermarkets had a great reputation with customers and employees and had just invested in a new format store in Yorba Linda, which became the new Vons store no. 69.

In January 1987, the first Tianguis store opened in Montebello, California. This 60,000-square-foot market was designed to cater to the specific needs of Hispanic customers. Tianguis, meaning "open-air marketplace" in Aztec, denotes a place where the community would meet to shop and socialize. The store offered an 11,000-square-foot produce department, a bottling plant for sweet drinks, a tortilleria for making fresh tortillas, and a salchichoneria for making over two dozen varieties of fresh sausages. All employees were bilingual, and signage in the stores was in both English and Spanish.

In July 1987, Vons merged with Allied Supermarkets Inc., a Detroit-based public company listed under the New York Stock Exchange. At the time of the merger, the new company was named The Vons Companies, and the Detroit operations were sold. This enabled Vons to become a publicly traded company.

In 1988, Vons acquired the Southern California operation of Safeway Stores from Kohlberg Kravis and Roberts and integrated them into The Vons Companies. The $408-million deal almost doubled the number of Vons stores and clearly placed Vons at number one in the nation's supermarket market.

Ken Doyle began his career with Vons in 1952, when it was a chain of just 19 stores and had just 1,000 employees. What he liked most about the company was the philosophy set by Charles, Ted, Wil, and Walter Von der Ahe that you "care for your people and hire the kind of people who care for others." Doyle was the perennial officer of the Vons Employee 4-U Fund that raised over $250,000 to assist employees in need. Doyle, vice president of personnel and labor relations, is pictured here just before his retirement in 1980.

Vons created the Diamond Circle and Golden Circle awards to recognize store managers who achieved a level of controllable profits well beyond the average store. Winners of the 1981 Golden Circle award pictured here are, from left to right, (first row) John Wahlrab, John Alexander, Gary Miller, and Bill Doty; (second row) Bill Lacey, Jim Braheem, Mike Gardiner, Gary Posey, Mel Balfour, Ken Bensen, Tom Kelly, John Gutheil, and Ken Neuharth.

In February 1981, Bud Moorman (left) was recognized as Retailer of the Year by the Southern California Deli Council. Here, Moorman is being presented with the award by Bob Arciniaga, chairman of the committee that selected Retailer and Supplier of the Year. Moorman also served as the president of the Southern California Deli Council in 1976. When he won this award, Moorman had been with Vons for over 30 years and was the head deli buyer.

In 1981, Vons acquired the Snowflake Bakery in San Diego. The bakery was purchased to aid Vons central bakery in the production of buns and bread. Many Vons executives, including Dick Risher, Bob Hearn, and Dick London, gathered at a luncheon to welcome the 70 new employees into the Vons family. Pictured here are, from left to right, Jesse Esparaza, plant supervisor; Ken Olsen; Thelma Voornees, office manager; Jerry Fahey; Ted Borland, plant manager; Richard Lumsden, chief engineer; and Jose Vasquez, sanitation foreman.

Because location is so important in retail, prior to Vons entering the Fresno market, a team of Vons executives toured various sites in Fresno and Visalia in June 1982 for the optimum placement of up to six stores. On this day, the developer flew members of the executive team to Visalia to show them the last few potential sites for the Visalia store. Pictured here are, from left to right, Ken Olsen, Dick London, Glen Oltmanns, and Don Howard.

Vons hosted Hawaiian Days, an annual event in which all store employees dressed in Hawaiian attire and all stores were decorated with a Hawaiian theme. Stores also did significant merchandising and sales related to the theme. Hawaiian Days also carried over to the main office. Pictured here are, from left to right, Jack Riedinger, Sonny King, Joe Raymond, Jan Dell, Kay Griffin, and Dick Guilds.

Vons hosted an annual holiday party for the members of the corporate office. The party was held in the first-floor lunchroom in the main office, and Bill Madison and his deli kitchen team provided an extravaganza that included lobster and prime rib. Included in this photograph from the early 1980s are Virginia Acierni, Dorothy Hamilton, Joyce Bryant, Mary Bray, Bonnie Gabler, Moe Lemons, and Donna Kauffman.

Enjoying the feast prepared by Bill Madison for the holiday party are, from left to right, Bonnie Gabler, Jim McCloud, Bonnie Diener, Cecilia Martinez, Mitchell Crawford, and Ken Smith.

Jack Brennan was a general merchandise buyer in the corporate office and was widely respected in the general merchandise industry. On this day in 1981, Brennan returned to his office to find that his friends had decorated his office in honor of his "over the hill" birthday.

This c. 1982 photograph shows members of the Vons human resources team. Pictured are, from left to right, (first row) Judy Barnhill, Loree Rice, Diane Lugo, Mary Jane Herron, and Midge Young; (second row) Sally Berg, Barbara Charles, Rose Glenn, Rae Campbell, Barney McCallum, and Norma Kentner; (third row) Fred Piethman, Dick Risher, Bill Heinen, Mike Stark, and Skip Adams; (fourth row) Gary Duncan, Bill Gensmere, Roy Rute, Jim Dunbar, and Bob Hearn.

In 1982 Vons experimented with other formats when converting Vons store no. 81 in Long Beach to a warehouse-style discount supermarket. This was Vons' first venture into alternative food retailing. Pictured here are, from left to right, Ben Harrington, Don Howard, Ron Scott, Tom ?, Jeff Hendges, Joe Shasha, Floyd Hall, and George Stanley.

In 1954, Vons formed a credit union called the Vons Employees Federal Credit Union. It served many Vons employees with services typically provided by a bank. The first branch of the credit union was in the corporate office; it later moved to the south end of the Vons Distribution Center and then, in 1983, to its own office on Arden Way. In 1983, the credit union had 16,000 members and $24 million in assets. At right is a listing of the savings and loan interest rates for the credit union in 1983.

INTEREST RATES on SAVINGS ACCOUNTS *(rates subject to change)*	
Share Accounts	7% APR
Share Draft Accounts	6% APR
Ultra Account	15% APR
Six Month Money Market Certificates	8.89% APR
30 Month Certificates	9.75% APR
13 Month Certificates	7.5% APR
Fixed IRA Account	9.75% APR
Variable Rate IRA Accounts	11.5% APR
INTEREST RATES on LOANS	
Car Loans-New	
36 months	12% APR
48 months	15% APR
60 months	18% APR
Car Loans-Used	15% APR
Motorcycle Loans	18% APR
Second Trust Deed/Home Improvement Loans	18% APR
Bill Consolidation Loans	15% APR
Signature Loans	15% APR
Share Secured Loan	10.8% APR
Express Loans	15% APR

Vons Employees Federal Credit Union employees pictured here are, from left to right, (first row) Betty Hearn, Minnie ?, Jeanne Christensen, Cindy Ehlinger, Guynell More, Darlene Dobbs, Terry Janke, and Peggy Carner; (second row) president and chief executive officer Skip Adams, Cheri Malek, Andrea Cox, Shirley Komen, Cheryl Voss, and Bonnie Barrett.

Starting in the summer of 1980 and continuing for six years, different members of Vons management took a horseback pack trip, organized by Mike Stark, to the Eastern Sierra. For some, like Dave Llewellyn, it was their first time camping in the backcountry, but the great experiences and friendship would last a life time. Others who made the trek included Harold Anderson, Jerry Scorsatto, Joe Lemire, Larry Jahr, and Ed Marrujo. Pictured here are district managers Jerry Stotko (left) and Jesse Malone. (Courtesy of Michael Stark.)

In 1982, Grey Advertising, Vons' advertising agency, recognized Vons for attaining $2 billion in sales. Grey Advertising had a longstanding relationship with Vons and was behind the creation of many of the very successful advertising campaigns, such as "Double the Difference" and "The Karate Price Slasher." These campaigns set Vons apart from the rest of the industry. In this image, Carol Naylon, senior vice president at Grey, is presenting Ken Olsen with a commemorative award. Pictured are, from left to right, Bill Davila, Jerry Fahey, Olsen, Naylon, and Miles Turpin (executive vice president at Grey).

Members of the 1983 spring management training class pictured here are, from left to right, (first row) Bud Stoll, Paul Sheffield, Steve Klepach, Din Hansen, Pam Billings, Mike Flowers, Christopher Ryan, and Darrell Ortiz; (second row) Chuck McCoy, Greg Stark, Russ Parker, Gary Bean, Hitoshi Snyder, training manager Wendy Hodkinson, Bill Roth, Jeff Moors, Ken West, Mark Wright, and Roy Hays; (third row) Don Holt, Jim Loper, Dave Eaton, Chuck Russo, Brian Murphy, Chris Glover, and Bryan Carlton.

Barbara Organ and Anne Schmidt decorate the steer head located on the wall in Bob Kelly's office in the meat service center. The steer head became the center of attention for a variety of pranks and jokes at different times of the year. This time, it appears to have a Hawaiian Days theme, but the head was also decorated for Cinco de Mayo, the Fourth of July, and the Christmas holiday season.

Depicting important events in the history of Vons Grocery Company, this illustration was commissioned to commemorate the retirement of Vons president Ken Olsen as a tribute to him and past presidents for their dedication and vision in making Vons a great company. The lithograph was numbered in a limited edition.

These 1983 recipients of the University of Southern California Food Industry Management program scholarships are Bob Dyer (left), former store manager at Vons store no. 7 and on special assignment to assist Joe Raymond, vice president of sales; Susan Lawmaster (center), a computer programmer; and Bud Stoll, grocery manager at Vons store no. 25. Each of the scholarships, valued at approximately $8,000, were provided by various food industry suppliers.

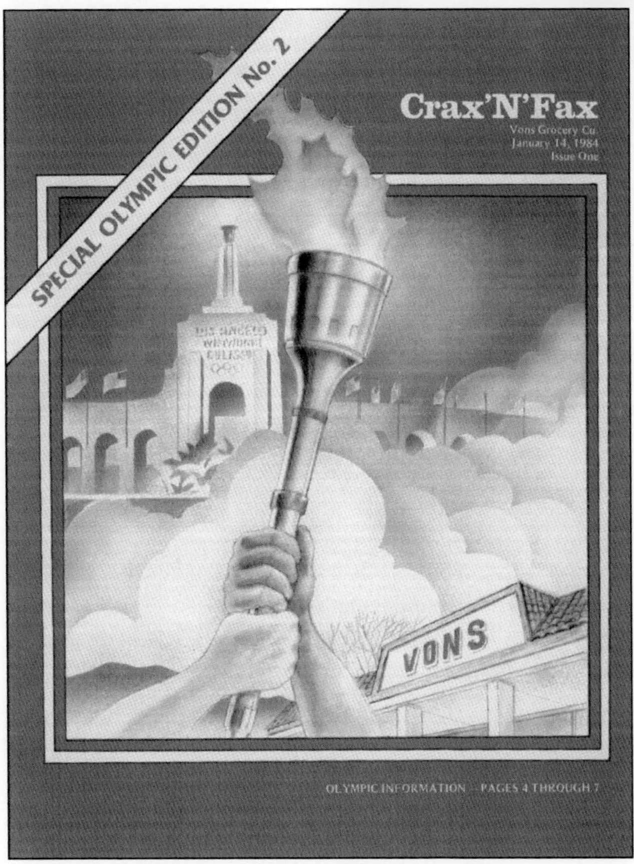

In January 1984, Vons announced to the world that they were the official food sponsors for the 1984 Summer Olympic Games in Los Angeles. This was a tremendous achievement for Vons and would provide them with an unparalleled marketing opportunity. As history indicates, the games and Vons' marketing efforts were a huge success! Ken Olsen started this effort in 1983, following a phone call from Peter Ueberroth, and worked with Jerry Fahey and the Vons executive team to create an unequaled, historic event for Vons.

Bob Hadeler held a number of executive-level positions in distribution and logistics. Under his leadership, Vons' supply-chain processes were taken to a new level of efficiency. Pictured at Hadeler's retirement in 1984 are Steve Weakley (left), Hadeler, and Barbara Giovanni Baisley.

On February 29, 1988, the Duke and Duchess of York, Prince Andrew and Sarah Ferguson (right), paid a royal visit to Pavilions store no. 208 in Arcadia. Upon arrival, they were greeted by a crowd of more than 300 people who braved the cold and rain to see them. They were escorted through the store by Roger Stangeland and Bill Davila (left).

Pictured at an industry function are, from left to right, Joe Raymond, vice president of sales, and his wife, JoAnne, with Wil Von der Ahe and his wife, Mary Jane.

Members of the 1987 management training class pictured here are, from left to right, (first row) Jim McMahon, Mike Romero, Dave Jones, Jim Manseau, Jim Vitellli, Joe Flaco, Richard Beserra, and Ed Bennett; (second row); training manager Tom Gilmore, Al Andersen, Kathy Lotz, Greg Santos, Dan Barth, Steve Delgado, John Spohn, Vince Eichten, Tebbi Dugan, and training specialist John Henshaw; (third row), Darrell Turner, Dan Spain, Mike Young, Steve Hager, Doug Dill, Dan Agostini, and Jim Kuykendall.

Members of the Vons Store Management T.E.A.M. Training pictured here are, from left to right, unidentified, Terry Collier, Natalie De Ulloa, Wendy Kennedy, John Henshaw, and Steve Taylor.

Wil Von der Ahe and his wife, Mary Jane, are pictured here shortly after Wil's retirement from Vons.

Five

Restructuring Years 1990–1997

The early 1990s saw the introduction of two new store formats—Expo, the warehouse club format that was abandoned in 1995, and the super combo format, which included banking services, catering facilities, a dry cleaner, photograph processing, a pharmacy, and an expanded grocery section. Later in the decade, the super combo format was essentially melded into the Vons and Pavilions formats.

In January 1992, Vons acquired family-owned Williams Brothers Markets, located in central California. The 18-store chain was well known for customer service and tailoring their offerings to local communities. They integrated well with other stores in the Vons portfolio while allowing Vons to expand further north.

In 1994, Larry Del Santo returned to Vons as vice chairman and chief executive officer. Joining Del Santo as president and chief operating officer was Dick Goodspeed, who also worked with Del Santo at Lucky Stores. Under Del Santo's leadership, the company's focus became maintaining its aggressive promotional position in the Southern California market, introducing the upscale Pavilions format in San Diego, and continuing to empower employees to keep the fun in selling. Del Santo related in a September 1996 interview in *Supermarket News* that "being a preferred employer goes back to the premise that we can't be a good place to shop without first being a good place to work."

In attempts to mark Vons as a "preferred employer," Del Santo replaced the term "employee" with "associate" to foster a culture of inclusion and empowerment. The "Straight from the Heart" program was created to empower associates to take care of a customer's needs. Around the same time, a mentoring program was established to develop associates who had high potential for promotion to store manager. Del Santo recognized that it took great leaders to lead a great company and invested in the success of future Vons leaders.

Another initiative undertaken by Del Santo and Goodspeed included letting increased volume drive productivity and bottom-line results. They implemented the recommendations of seven task forces focusing on labor productivity, store format evolution, in-store merchandising, category-based merchandising, logistics, real estate, and manufacturing, which impacted operations for years to come.

In 1996, Vons added 12 new stores to its chain, including four bought from Smith's Food & Drug. Late that year, the company was making plans to open 12 to 15 stores in 1997—six of them Pavilions, including the first San Diego stores for that format. Around this time, Safeway offered to purchase the 65 percent of Vons that it did not already own. The deal was completed in April 1997, with Safeway paying about $2.5 billion to complete the purchase, including $565 million in debt. Vons thereby became a wholly-owned subsidiary of Safeway, but its 320 stores continued to operate under the Vons and Pavilions names. This acquisition created the nation's second-largest supermarket chain, with 1,377 stores throughout the United States. On the date of the announcement, the price of a share of Vons stock jumped from $4.53 to $53.50.

Vons continues to operate in Southern California as a successful division of Safeway Inc.

The new store formats proved to be successful for Vons. Considerable research into customer demographics and shopping habits were behind the development of the Pavilions and Tianguis formats. Start-up teams were established, and the members traveled across the United States and to other countries to visit other supermarket chains with unique departments and product offerings. This photograph of the service deli department in one of the Pavilion stores demonstrates a considerable change from the deli departments in the early stores.

Vons expanded their prepared food offerings beyond merely cheese and meat platters. In this advertisement, they marketed a variety of prepared food for parties, letting customers know they could leave the work to Vons and spend time enjoying the party. Pictured in this advertisement is Bonnie Gabler Petralia, a member of the Vons advertising department.

Vons worked with Dr. Brian Harris, an industry consultant, to introduce the competency of category management. This involved processes for increasing sales by trading up, selling tie-ins, or cross-merchandising. It was a new philosophy for the industry, because buyers historically only managed warehouse inventory without mind to carrying costs; now, category managers owned the carrying costs of inventory from cradle to grave. The first category management training class is pictured here in 1990; they are, from left to right, (first row) Kim Fella (industry consultant), Rodney Boshard, Raymond Swain, Claudia Reich, Mark De Bruin, Paul Knerr, Diane Babinski, Pat Defreeze, Jim Poe, and Kent Kuwata; (second row) Dr. Brian Harris, Harold Rudnick, Doug Ratto, John Mas, Dale Fowler, Donna Harris, Michelle Eastman, Bernice Grieve, Joe Flaco, Jim Wakefield, Dave Brennan, and Mike Schall (industry consultant); (third row) Bill Gensemer, Harvey Durand, Joe Damiano, Dan Graham, Brenda Russo, Don Bandow, Jim O'Bryant, Tracy Wolpert, Bill Tarter, Jerry Scorsatto, and Bob Hodgin (Coca-Cola representative); (fourth row) Larry Ishii, Pam Billings, Russ Hoffman, Terry Clothier, Frank Neal, Bill Roth, Jack Brennan, Cliff Lovelace, Nick Alex, John Caruso, Jim Pearson, and Randy Golden.

This is a carniceria, the full-service meat department at a Tianguis store in Montebello. Note the hanging beef and meat-trimming tools in the background, which allowed meat department associates to prepare custom cuts of beef for customers.

To outperform the competition in the tough Southern California marketplace, store managers were required to use innovative tactics in employee relations, merchandising, and problem solving. In 1994, *Progressive Grocer* recognized 24 Vons store managers for doing this. Pictured on the cover of *Crax'N'Fax* is Bob Erickson, store manager at store no. 179 in Alhambra. Erickson was recognized for tailoring his store's offerings to appeal to the ever-growing Asian population in the San Gabriel Valley. His goal was to be the best Asian food–merchandised store in the entire country.

Here, Bill and Dorothy Davila relax at a Vons event in 1992. Bill retired as president of Vons in 1992 but continued on as president emeritus and acted as company spokesperson on all company radio, television, and print advertising. For a time in the late 1980s, Bill was one of the most recognizable television personalities in Los Angeles due to his appearance in Vons television commercials. (Courtesy of Dorothy Davila.)

Bill Davila's retirement party, held at the Pasadena Civic Auditorium, was attended by many industry executives and celebrities. Michael Feinstein played the piano, and Vikki Carr sang in Davila's honor. More than 1,000 people attended the celebration and dinner. Attending the black-tie event were, from left to right, Barbara Hartel, Barbara Giovanni-Baisley, Rosemarie Palamino, and Sharon Westover.

Pete Horn (left), group vice president of operations, is congratulating John Spohn (right), store manager, on receiving his 25-year-anniversary gold watch at the annual 1992 service awards dinner at the Warner Center Marriott. As the company and the number of employees grew, the service awards events were held regionally, typically in the Central Valley, Los Angeles, and San Diego. (Courtesy of John Spohn.)

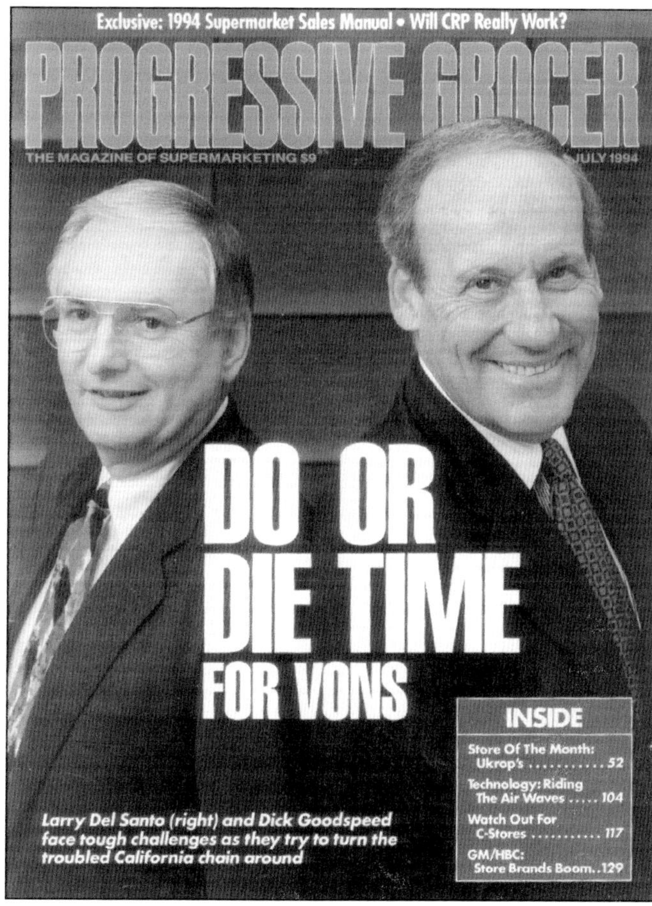

In 1994, Larry Del Santo (right) returned to Vons as vice-chairman and chief executive officer from American Stores Company Inc., where he was senior vice president and chief operating officer. Dick Goodspeed (left), chief operating officer at American Stores Company Inc., came with Del Santo as president and chief operating officer. At that time, Vons had been suffering the effects of the recession, as well as a number of other factors that had depressed company revenue. Peers in the industry recognized that the combination of these two experienced grocery executives could make a significant difference at Vons and in the industry.

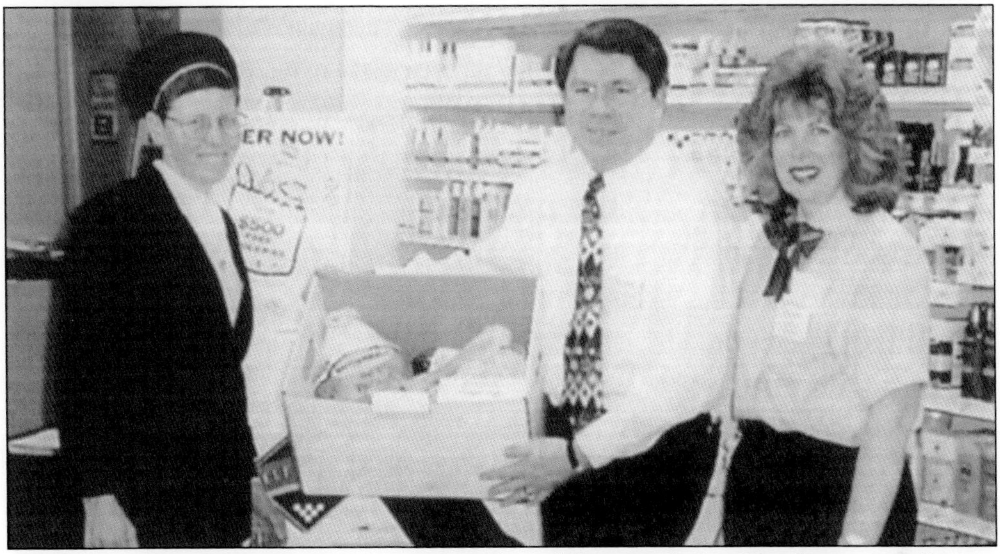

Pavilions store no. 233 in Los Angeles got into the holiday spirit before Thanksgiving, collecting cash to buy Thanksgiving dinners for the homeless at the Sisters of Rolling Hills shelter. They were able to collect enough money to pay for 20 dinners. "This was one thing that we could do as a store that helped a good cause and made us all feel good," said Debbie Rozas, senior supervisor, in a *Crax'N'Fax* article. Pictured here are an unidentified member of the Sisters of Rolling Hills (left), Mike Courtis (center), and Rozas.

Vons store no. 72 in Ventura asked customers to vote for their four "Friendliest Vons Associates"—the winning associates would have their names posted and earn prizes. One of the winning associates was Cyndy Roberts, pictured here with a happy customer in the January 1997 edition of *Vons Ink*.

In November 1996, when a customer came into store no. 72 to pick up a Thanksgiving dinner, the dinner was missing. After trying to come up with a solution, Irma Lopez, the service deli clerk, generously offered her own Vons turkey dinner. "Irma put our customer's needs ahead of her own," said Terry Richardson, district manager. As thanks for her generosity, Irma was rewarded with a special Christmas dinner for her and her family. Pictured here are assistant store manager Tom Fardig (left), Lopez, and Richardson.

Pavilions stores nos. 209 (Lakewood), 215 (Thousand Oaks), and 240 (Fullerton) lent a hand to Children's Hospital of Orange County at their annual Pediatric Cancer Research Foundation Roundup in 1996. The stores ran two game booths and barbecued hamburgers and hot dogs. Store managers Nick Stefano and Rob McDougal brought their families, who also assisted with the event.

District 9 associates held a fundraising golf tournament for three associates, all of whom had cancer. The tournament was organized by Phil Tucker, district manager, and District 9 store managers. The associates who received checks for $1,500 were Valerie Elias (left), from Vons store no. 76 in Long Beach; Elizabeth Bustamante (right), from Vons store no. 25 in Lakewood; and Anthony Miller (center), from Pavilions store no. 519 in Long Beach.

Vons and the United Food and Commercials Workers Union united to raise nearly $80,000 for the Leukemia Society. Pictured here are, from left to right, Brian Dowling (director of public affairs), Roy Hays (district manager), Donna Lunch (Leukemia Society), and an unidentified young leukemia patient and his father. "This is just one of many examples of just how Vons associates show their 'heart' both in and out of work," said Hays in a *Vons Ink* interview.

Members of the Vons mixed relay team competed in the 1994 Jimmy Stewart Relay Marathon and finished in first place in the supermarket division mixed-team category. Pictured here are, from left to right, Roy Ituralde, Vons store no. 300; Diane Graham and Julie Hiramatsu, Vons store no. 301; Paul Rodriguez, Vons store no. 300; and Bryan Allen, loss prevention.

In 1995, Prince Charles visited the United States on a tour to promote British foods. One of his stops was at Vons, where he and his entourage visited a Pavilions store and met with Larry Del Santo and other members of the Vons executive team.

Leaders of the some of the major Southern California grocery companies posed for this photograph at a grocery-industry-sponsored charity event. Pictured in 1996, from left to right, are Kevin Davis, Bristol Farms president; Byron Allumbaugh, Ralphs chief executive officer; Al Marasca, Ralphs president and chief operating officer; Jack Brown, Stater Bros. chairman and chief executive officer; Larry Del Santo, Vons chairman and chief executive officer; Bill Davila, Vons president emeritus; Dick Goodspeed, Vons president and chief operating officer; and Don Baker, Stater Bros. president and chief operating officer. (Courtesy of Dorothy Davila.)

In a unique campaign to promote the use of the Vons Card, Vons provided an opportunity for one of its customers to win $1,000,000 by swiping their Vons Club card. Bill Davila presented the winner with the first check for $50,000 and pledged a commitment to pay another $50,000 each year for 20 years.

At the 1997 company holiday party are, from left to right, (seated) John and Joanne Reyburn, Lisa and David Lee, and George and Peggy Boyle; (standing) Jerry and Susan Scorsatto, Terry and Diane Peets, and Dorothy and Bill Davila. (Courtesy of George Boyle.)

Volume 46, Number 45 $6.00

SN

Supermarket News Monday, November 4, 1996

Safeway Offers $1.6 Billion In Stock to Acquire Vons

By ELLIOT ZWIEBACH

PLEASANTON, Calif. — In a bid to continue fattening its earnings, Safeway here last week proposed to acquire Vons Cos., Arcadia, Calif., for about $1.65 billion in stock.

Vons' management, apparently caught off-guard by the unsolicited merger proposal, said Safeway's offer "will be studied by a committee of outside directors of Vons, which will respond in due course." Safeway gave Vons two weeks to respond. Observers said if Vons agrees to the proposal, a merger would be unlikely before early spring.

The merger would add Vons' 325 stores and $5 billion in 1995 sales to Safeway's 1,050 units and 1995 sales of $16.4 billion, boosting Safeway from the third-largest U.S. chain to No. 2, with sales of $21.4 billion — behind Kroger's $23.9 billion but ahead of American Stores' $18.3 billion. In stating the volume of the combined operations last week, Safeway used a figure of $22.5 billion, which it said was based on the chains' combined sales for the last 12 months.

Safeway's terms involve a stock-for-stock merger in which each share of Vons' common stock Safeway doesn't own would be exchanged, tax free, for 1.34 shares of Safeway common stock. Safeway also would assume $600 million of Vons' debt on top of its existing indebtedness of $1.8 billion, said Steve Burd,

Continued on Page 67

Safeway's Steve Burd said he expected Vons to react positively.

Vons' Dick Goodspeed would head Safeway's Vons division after a merger.

On October 30, 1996, Safeway announced that it had made an offer to acquire Vons for about $1.65 billion in stock. Vons management commented that the offer would be studied by a committee of outside directors. At the time, Vons had 325 stores and $5 billion in sales. The merger would result in Safeway having 1,375 stores and $21.4 billion in sales, moving Safeway to number two, behind Kroger. On the day of the announcement, the price of Vons' shares rose from $11.22 to $54.34. The merger was completed in early 1997.

Six

Vons Senior Leadership 1906–1997

One thing that truly made Vons a special place to work and differentiated it from other companies was the leadership style of the management team. Starting at the very top, Vons leadership continually instilled a customer service philosophy throughout the company.

From the beginning, when Charles Von der Ahe first created his vision, he recognized that understanding the needs of the customer was the top priority. Moreover, he realized that instilling this culture throughout the organization was essential and would be the key to their success.

Since that time, and under the leadership of all of Von der Ahe's successors, Vons continued to focus on customer expectations of great service and value and ensured that this was executed at all levels of the company. Training and development programs focusing on the customer and excellent execution were always included in annual plans to reinforce this philosophy. Upward mobility was a reward for those who carried on this tradition.

The leaders of the company included innovators who significantly influenced the grocery industry with creative new store concepts (such as Pavilions and Tianguis), new efficiency processes (such as Total Store Scheduling, Category Management and Straight from the Heart), and innovative marketing (such as Double the Difference, double and triple coupons, and the Vons Card).

Another area that differentiated Vons was the company's reputation as a great place to work. People always wanted to join the company. Vons leadership recognized that when you could offer a promising career, you received, in return, a high level of commitment and sense of ownership from your employees that translated into improved execution and customer service.

The following chapter is dedicated to those who served as Vons senior executives over the decades and who continued the early traditions of Charles and the entire Von der Ahe family.

They Started it All
The Von der Ahes

The roots of the Vons Grocery Company go back to Copenhagen, Denmark, where Charles Von der Ahe was born. His parents emigrated to the United States when Charles was a young boy. As a teen, he worked as a delivery boy for a combination meat shop and grocery store in Alton, Illinois. It soon became apparent that the grocery business was in his blood. He moved out west and worked for several markets in San Francisco, Arizona, and Los Angeles before opening his first market on Seventh and Figueroa Streets in 1906. He met and married his boss's daughter, Linda Lauer, of the meatpacking family, in 1907. The store was a family business, and Linda worked as the store's first checker, taking phone orders from most of the customers. While Linda and Charles were building a successful grocery store chain, they were also raising a family of eight children. Two of those children, Ted and Wil, steered the family-run business even after the company was acquired by Household Finance Corporation. Another son, Walter, supervised the personnel functions of the company for many years before striking out on his own. This photograph shows Vons' original leadership team; they are, from left to right, Walter, Wil, Charles, and Ted. The Von der Ahes set the standard of excellence for years to come.

Charles Von der Ahe opened the first Vons store in 1906 in downtown Los Angeles. By 1928, he had developed a food chain of 87 stores, which he sold that year to McMarr Stores. The year 1932 marked the beginning of the present-day Vons, when Charles, along with his sons Ted and Wil, opened a new Vons store no. 1 in Lynwood. The company prospered, and in the ensuing years, Charles and his sons guided Vons through dynamic years of startling growth to build one of the strongest, most respected food chains in the country. Charles was a prominent figure in Southern California business and philanthropic organizations. He was a past president of the Western Association of Food Chains (WAFC) and the Southern California Grocers Association. He served as president of the LA Breakfast Club and Brothers Club and as director of the Wilshire Country Club. Charles served on the Board of St. John of God Hospital and, in 1957, was named a knight commander of St. Gregory by special proclamation of Pope Pius XII. He was also a major contributor to the Von der Ahe Memorial Library, which was constructed at Loyola University of Los Angeles in 1959.

Ted Von der Ahe learned the grocery business from the ground up by sweeping floors, waiting on customers, and running errands in the early stores owned by his father, Charles. When Ted was starting out in grocery in the early 1930s, the country was suffering through the Depression, so Ted and his brother Wil decided to put their energies into the family business. After working in every operation of the company, Ted assumed the role of president of Vons in 1956, a position he held until 1973. Ted retired from Vons in 1976. In addition to his activities in the grocery industry, Ted's business savvy and expertise was sought out by many other corporations. He was on the boards of directors for Bank of America, Household Finance, National Association of Food Chains, and Farmers Insurance Group. Ted's philanthropic efforts were also extensive and included the City of Hope, the Catholic Welfare Bureau, and active involvement with Our Little Brothers and Sisters, an orphanage and school in Cuernavaca, Mexico.

Like his brother Ted, Wil Von der Ahe learned the business from his dad, Charles. Wil eventually became executive vice president, chairman of the executive committee, and a member of the board of directors of Vons before retiring in 1976. As cofounder of a chain of supermarkets that started with one small grocery department, Wil did everything in the store. This included running newly acquired outside departments and closing at night. In 1949, when there were about 16 stores in the chain and about 500 employees, Charles, Ted, and Wil comprised "upper management." Wil was in charge of store operations and the grocery department. Later, as the company branched out, he also took on responsibility for site development and new store construction. Over the years, many innovative fixtures and store designs were created by Wil. Wil, like his brother, was also involved in community work. He served on numerous boards, including the advisory board of St. Joseph's Hospital in Burbank, the board of directors of Holy Cross Hospital in Northridge, the board of regents of Santa Clara University, and the board of trustees of Loyola Marymount University. Wil was also president of the Western Association of Food Chains, vice president of the National Association of Food Chains, president of the California Grocers Association, vice president and director of the Supermarket Institute, and director of the Food Employers Council.

Lawrence (Larry) A. Del Santo began his career with Vons in 1958 after graduating from college and serving in the military. His first position was as a trainee in the advertising department, and he subsequently assumed the positions of vice president of advertising and then marketing. He quickly rose to become president and chief executive officer of Vons. In 1974, Del Santo was chosen by Household International, Vons' parent company, to lead the city products division, of which Vons was a subsidiary. In 1984, Del Santo left city products to become president of Lucky Stores, which was purchased by American Stores Company Inc. in 1989. In 1994, Del Santo returned to Vons as chairman and chief executive officer; he retired in 1997 following Vons acquisition by Safeway. He has served on various boards, including those of SuperValu, PetSmart, and A.G. Ferrari Foods. He also served as a trustee of the University of San Francisco and the Tomas Rivera Center. He was a director of the Los Angeles Area Chamber of Commerce, Criminal Justice Legal Foundation, Los Angeles Business Advisors, and the Food Marketing Institute. (Courtesy of Larry Del Santo.)

Ken Olsen began his career with Vons in 1946 in the meat department. He moved up the ranks to meat department manager, meat division supervisor, and, in 1959, became division manager. In 1965, Olsen assumed the responsibilities of sales and merchandising manager, and was appointed manager of store operations in 1967. In January 1970, Olsen was promoted to the position of vice president and general manager. In 1973, he was named to senior vice president and, the following year, was appointed to executive vice president. He was then promoted to president and chief executive officer in September 1975 until his retirement in 1984. Olsen was instrumental in working with Peter Ueberroth in establishing Vons as the main food supplier to the 1984 Summer Olympics in Los Angeles. Olsen is a past president of the Western Association of Food Chains (WAFC) and past director of the Food Marketing Institute. In 1984, Ken was presented with the coveted Sidney R. Rabb Award, the food industry's highest award. He is also a past member of the LA Better Business Bureau and vice chair of the LA Area Chamber of Commerce. His association with charitable organizations includes the California Adoption Foundation, Little Sisters of the Poor, Big Brothers of America, and the LA Rotary Club. Ken was a regent of Loyola Marymount University, a knight commander of St. Gregory the Great, and a knight of the Sovereign Military Order of St. John of Jerusalem of Rhodes and Malta.

Jerry Fahey started his Vons career in 1954 as a produce clerk and worked his way up to produce division manager in 1965. In 1971, he was promoted to sales and merchandising manager, then to vice president of marketing in 1973. In 1975, Fahey was named executive vice president and chief operating officer. In 1983, Fahey became president and chief executive officer. In 1984, he retired from Vons for only one year, then went to work for Lucky Stores in 1985 as vice president of marketing for the Northern Food Division. He retired from Lucky Stores in 1990. When Fahey was named president, he expressed two main objectives—the first was to maintain the family spirit of Vons that the Von der Ahes established (as the first non-family president, this was very important to Jerry). The second was to continue Vons as a successful entity in the Household International family so they would continue to invest in the expansion of Vons. Fahey is past president of the Western Association of Food Chains, past advisor to the USC Food Industry Management Program, and industry chairman for the United Way and City of Hope. He also served as president of the Covina Police and Fire Building Commission, president of South Hills Country Club, and held leadership roles in several businesses outside of the food industry. (Courtesy of Jerry Fahey.)

In 1982, Roger Stangeland became a group executive at Household Merchandising, where Vons was one of the many Household International–owned companies that he oversaw. Two years later, Stangeland joined Vons as chairman and chief executive officer; the following year, he led a leveraged buyout to acquire the chain from its parent, Household Merchandising. The deal was one of the largest in the grocery industry at the time—and one of the most successful, according to industry analysts. It allowed Vons to make major acquisitions in the 1980s and to open multiple new grocery formats. Stangeland retired from his position as chief executive of Vons in 1994 and did a brief stint as chairman of the New Jersey–based Grand Union before leaving the grocery business. However, he continued to serve on the Vons board until it the company was purchased by Safeway Inc. in 1997, and he served as chairman of the Food Marketing Institute. Stangeland served on the boards of directors of the Boy Scouts of America and the Los Angeles Chamber of Commerce and was a member of the board of fellows of Claremont Graduate School. Stangeland was active in charity work, fundraising for Methodist Hospital and the Pasadena Playhouse, where he was a director, as well as St. John's Northwestern Military Academy, a college-prep school he fondly remembered.

Bill Davila began his 50 year career with Vons as an apprentice produce department clerk in 1948 and was promoted to produce department manager in 1956. In April 1959, Davila started working in Vons' advertising department and held various roles until his promotion to advertising and promotions manager in 1973. Following this, Davila held executive roles as vice president of sales, group vice president of marketing and sales, senior vice president of supermarketing, and executive vice president. In January 1985, Davila was named president and chief operating officer of The Vons Companies and remained in this role until his retirement in April 1992. Following his retirement, Davila went on to serve as Vons president emeritus from 1992 through 1998, acting as Vons' chief spokesperson and remaining on Vons' board of directors. For many years, Davila was a star on Southern California television due to his leading role in the Vons television commercials. At one time, he was one of the most recognized television personalities in the region. Davila served as a member of the boards of directors for Geo. A. Hormel & Company, Home Depot Inc., the Pacific Gas and Electric Company (where he was a member of the audit committee), and for Wells Fargo & Company. He also served as the chairman of the California Office of Traffic. (Courtesy of Dorothy Davila.)

Dennis Eck served as Vons president and chief operating officer from May 1994 to November 1996. Currently, Dennis is the interim chief executive officer for Ulta Salon, Cosmetics & Fragrance Inc. Prior to this recent appointment, he served as non-executive chairman of the board of directors and a director of Ulta Beauty since 2003. Dennis held various executive roles with Coles Myer, one of Australia's largest retailers, from 1994 to 2001. He was chief executive officer and a member of the board of Coles Myer LTD Australia from November 1997 to September 2001. Prior to 1994, Eck served in various executive roles with American Stores Company Inc., including as chairman of American Food and Drug, a subsidiary of American Stores Company Inc., and also served as its chief executive officer from 1987 to February 1990 and president from 1987 to 1988. Dennis also held positions as president and chief operating officer of Acme Markets Inc. and senior vice president of marketing from 1984 to 1985.

Dick Goodspeed joined Vons as president and chief operating officer in 1994, when Larry Del Santo returned to Vons as chairman and chief executive officer. Goodspeed later became Vons' chief executive officer and remained in this role until his retirement in 1998. Before his retirement, Goodspeed spent 45 years in all areas of retail management at some of the nation's largest and most successful grocery chains. He spent the last nine years working as a consultant for a variety of food retailers and consumer packaged goods companies. Prior to his consulting assignments and his role at Vons, Goodspeed spent 37 years in various management positions at Lucky Stores, the last eight of which were as president and chief operating officer at American Stores Company Inc., and four years at the Great Atlantic and Pacific Tea Company, including a year as president of Family Mart Stores. Goodspeed was active in a number of food industry associations and community organizations, including serving as a director of the Food Marketing Institute, president of the Western Association of Food Chains, and on the board of directors of the Boy Scouts of America, Bay Area Council. He was also named executive of the year by the Food Industry Management Program at the University of Southern California and currently serves as a director on various corporate boards, including as the first non-shareholder to serve as the chairman of Unified Grocers. (Courtesy of Dick Goodspeed.)

Seven

THE SPIRIT OF VONS 2009 AND 2011

This book captures the historical timeline from 1906 through the purchase of Vons by Safeway Inc. in 1997, but the "spirit of Vons" clearly lives on!

In recognition of this, current and former Vons employees gathered at two Vons reunions. The first was in September 2009 at the Pacific Palms Resort (formerly the Sheraton Industry Hills), a venue for many past Vons events. A reunion committee formed by a number of former Vons associates knew that such a reunion would be a huge success. The committee—organized in March 2009 and chaired by Wendy Kennedy and Mike Stark—included members Cel (Martinez) Avila, Barbara (Giovanni) Baisley, Mitchell and Suzy Crawford, Mary McAboy Del Santo, Russ Doyle, Harriet Maldonado, Bonnie (Gabler) Petralia, and Denise Vest.

Over 300 current and former Vons employees and guests gathered to share memories and reminisce about "great times" at Vons. Four former company presidents attended the reunions—Larry Del Santo, Ken Olsen, Jerry Fahey, and Dick Goodspeed. The former presidents shared their memories of leading the company and discussed some of the significant events in Vons history. They credited Vons' success to the dedicated employees—past and present—who care for their customers and for each other. Some of the attendees had been retired for more than 25 years and were reunited with friends whom they had not seen in years. Without exception, all in attendance were proud to have worked for such a great company and had a nice afternoon celebrating that time.

The second reunion, organized in 2011, was prompted by a comment by Ken Olsen after the 2009 reunion. Olsen commented to Stark that he hoped that "we" would do this again, as it was such an enjoyable afternoon; Stark responded that this was something to consider in five years. When Olsen reminded Stark that at 90 years of age, five years was a long time, Stark and the committee organized another reunion in 2011.

The following pictures most certainly confirm that the Vons spirit lives on!

VONS REUNION

(for current and former Vons management – office/administrative, facilities management and support staff employees who started their careers with Vons prior to 1997)

SUNDAY, SEPTEMBER 27, 2009

1:00 —6:00 P.M.

PACIFIC PALMS HOTEL & CONFERENCE CENTER

Our reunion will take place at the beautiful Pacific Palms (formerly Industry Hills Sheraton)

1 Industry Hills Parkway, City of Industry, CA 91744

(626) 810-4455

Special Room Rate $129.00, Golf Package $85.00 - Mention Vons Reunion

Cost: $55.00 per person. Lunch / No Host Bar

Dress Code: Nice Casual (No Shorts)

Adults Only Event

Due to interest and limited seating, reservations will be handled on a first come, first served basis.

Sorry, No Walk-Ins will be accommodated.

NOTE: This event is not sponsored or endorsed by Safeway Inc., The Vons Companies Inc., or any of their affiliates or subsidiaries.

——PLEASE TEAR HERE AND RETURN INFORMATION/RESERVATION FORM WITH YOUR CHECK——

Employee: ______________ Guest: ______________

Mailing Street Address: ______________

City/State/Zip: ______________

Telephone: (___) ______________ E-Mail ______________

Department Last Worked at Vons: ______________

Years Worked at Vons: From 19___ to ______

Reservations: ____ # person(s) @ $55.00 = $______

Make checks payable to: Vons Reunion

Mail to: REUNION c/o Cheryl Voss—Vons Credit Union, P.O. Box 8023, El Monte, CA 91734-2323

This invitation was sent to retirees to announce the reunion, which was scheduled to be held on September 27, 2009. (Courtesy of Susan Crawford.)

Members of the Vons reunion committee pictured here are, from left to right, Mary McAboy Del Santo, Mike Stark, Barbara (Giovanni) Baisley, Bonnie Petralia, Suzy Crawford, Harriet Maldonado, Cel (Martinez) Avila, Denise Vest, Russ Doyle, Wendy Kennedy, and Mitchell Crawford.

Pictured here are former president Dick Goodspeed (left); Lilah Stangeland (center), Roger Stangeland's spouse and VIP guest; and Sandra Goodspeed.

Pictured here are Dan and Barbara (Giovanni) Baisley (merchandising).

Pictured here are, from left to right, Cel (Martinez) Avila (promotions), Russ Doyle (non-retail procurement), and Pat Heflin (data entry).

Susan Scorsatto (promotions) and Jerry Scorsatto (vice president, merchandising) are pictured.

Pictured here, from left to right, are Mike Stark (store operations), Tracy Stark, Wendy Kennedy (training), and Jack Kennedy.

Pictured here are Sharon and Dick Maron (vice president of transportation).

Pictured here are Bonnie (general merchandise / health and beauty aids) and Rod Diener.

Pictured from left to right are Pranee Panitchuphon (inventory management), Diana Strowger (construction and maintenance), and Barbara Organ (president's office).

Pictured here are Dick Erskine (meat division), and Jeannie (Pointer) Erskine (*Crax'N'Fax*).

Pictured here are Bill Heinen (vice president of labor relations) and Nora Heinen.

Pictured here are, from left to right, Steve Weakley (president and chief executive officer of the Vons Employees Federal Credit Union), Jan Dell (development), and Mark McInerney (grocery product recovery).

Pictured here are, from left to right, Melanie Nable (corporate quality assurance), Ann Batiste (advertising), Jerry Scorsatto, Tita Baysa (advertising), and Sarah Barry (pricing).

Lucy and Glen Oltmanns (vice president of construction) are pictured in the foreground, while Steve Valance (store operations) is shown in the background.

These fine folks are, from left to right, Dave Llewellyn (store manager), John Caruso (Pavilions), and Chris Linskey (vice president of Tianguis).

Pictured here are, from left to right, Dan Baisley, Sandy Milon (GM/HBC), Don Hays (vice president of operations), and Barbara (Giovanni) Baisley.

Pictured here are, from left to right, Bill Davila Jr., Chris Linskey, Claudia Reich (marketing/advertising), Jo Ann Murdock (GM/HBA), and Tom Montano (marketing).

Larry Del Santo shared with the attendees some of the most memorable events during his two terms as president, including some of the interesting marketing campaigns that elevated Vons to number one in market share in the Southern California region.

Ken Olsen recalled his first days with Vons, working as a meat cutter after returning from World War II, and meeting his wife, Dickie. He also shared his memories of when Vons was selected as the major food provider to the 1984 Summer Olympic Games in Los Angeles.

Jerry Fahey recalled the importance that Vons placed on its people. He recognized that it was the commitment of Vons' employees that made it the successful company it grew to be. He further commented that it was a good place to work and have a nice career.

Dick Goodspeed recalled the opportunity he took to join Vons and work with Larry Del Santo to continue Vons' growth and success. Here, he is applauding the attendees for all their hard work and contributions to making Vons number one in the Southern California supermarket industry.

Following the presentation by each of the former presidents, a surprise guest was invited on stage to entertain the audience. She clearly surprised the former presidents, from left to right, Dick Goodspeed, Jerry Fahey, Ken Olsen, and Larry Del Santo. Former Vons associate Faye Haas (director of consumer affairs), dressed as Mae West and sang to the audience in full character, receiving a standing ovation at the conclusion of her performance. Below is a close-up photograph of Haas dressed as Mae West.

The four former presidents pictured here are, from left to right, Dick Goodspeed, Jerry Fahey, Ken Olsen, and Larry Del Santo.

Pictured here are Ken and Dickie Olsen.

Pictured here are Mary and Larry Del Santo.

Pictured here are Jerry and Alice Fahey.

Pictured here are Steve Weakley and Cheryl Voss, both from the Vons Employees Federal Credit Union.

Pictured here are Suzanne Dyer (public relations), and Robert Dyer (information resources).

Pictured here are Harriet Maldonado (left, president's office) and Mary McAboy Del Santo (vice president of investor relations).

Pictured here are Jim Wakefield (grocery marketing), and Natalie Sanders (grocery buying).

Pictured here are, from left to right, Bonnie (Gabler) Petralia (advertising), Tita Baysa, and Kitty Dunning (advertising).

Pictured here are, from left to right, Jerry Stotko (store operations), Janie Stotko, Suzanne May (store operations), and Brad Melvin (store operations).

Pictured here are, from left to right, John Turley (marketing), Leanne McKenzie (human resources), and Robert Dyer.

Pictured here are, from left to right, Jim McLaughlin (vice president of operations), Pat (Weimer) Hernandez (legal), and Judge Bill Birney (vice president and general counsel).

Pictured here are, from left to right, Sue (Lawmaster) Klug (vice president of marketing), Chris Linskey, Dan Granger (vice president of sales and marketing), Sonny King (vice president of the grocery division), and Tony King.

Pictured here are, from left to right, Ruuda (Carriere) Pender (human resources), Mike Stark, and Norma (Kentner) Risher (human resources).

Pictured here are, from left to right, Barbara (Giovanni) Baisley, Jerry Fahey, and Suzy Crawford (inventory management).

Pictured here are, from left to right, Chris Huff (store support), Lani Cassidy (electronic marketing), and Wendy and Jack Kennedy.

Pictured here are, from left to right, Carlene Clark (liquor buying office), Linda Bleach-Coupas (transportation), Diane Babinski (non-perishables marketing), Mary Davis (general liability), Frances Putnam (division pricing coordinator), Heather Princiotta (grocery buying), Barbara Hartel (corporate office), and Mike Princiotta (non-retail purchasing).

Pictured here are, from left to right, Denise Vest (bakery specialist), Dottie Hamilton (training), Dave Llewellyn, Jane Gallup, Frances Fernandez (human resources), Carol Smith (training), and Helene Robert (grocery buying office).

Pictured here are, from left to right, Suzy Crawford, Bonnie (Gabler) Petralia, Pat Heflin, Dee Favro (product promotions), Debra Bye (human resources), and Jeanne Thompson (data processing).

Pictured here are Patricia Riesgo (left, pharmacy), and Betty Wood (advertising).

Pictured here are Ken Olsen (left) and Gary Hammett (real estate).

Pictured are Craig and Louisa Bergner (advertising).

This photograph shows, from left to right, Barbara Organ, Denise Colombero (sales and marketing), Ted Rose, Karen Rose (electronic marketing), and Jo Natividad (finance).

Pictured here are Karen Fisher (left, procurement), Natalie Amick (center, electronic marketing), and Vickie Beck (GM/HBA).

Pictured are Claire Robert (left, meat office) and Armen Oghigian (logistics).

Pictured here are George "Lucky" Luciano (loss prevention) and his unidentified guest.

Pictured are Jacquie McAlpin (buying) and Mark McAlpin (construction).

Pictured here are, from left to right, (first row) Jane Gallup, Carol Smith, and Pat Chorbajian (training); (second row) Diane Mackey, Dottie Hamilton, Denise Vest, and May Nakano (training).

Pictured from left to right are LaVina Tetrow (operations), Val Haley (executive offices), and Harriet Maldonado.

Pictured clockwise, from front and center, are Bruce Stegmaier (consumer research), Helene Robert, Christine Ely (treasury), Christopher Ely, Steve Olman, Marie Olman (inventory management), Diane Babinski, Sharon Gresswell, Dick Gresswell (loss prevention), and Dee Favro.

Pictured here from left to right are Val Haley, Mary Davis, Robyn Hudspeth (VonsChek), Barbara Hartel, and Annette Williams.

Pictured here from left to right are Marci Turley (training), Carol Smith, Dottie Hamilton, and Pat Chorbajian. In the background, Jan Faller (accounts payable) is tearing off raffle tickets.

Pictured here from left to right are (seated) Bonzell Uko, Robert Mohn (produce buyer), Sherry Mohn, Mickey Dolleschel (transportation), Marshall Pierce (logistics), Vicki Gassaway (logistics), and Carlene Clark; (standing in the background at left) Lynn Reyes-Trujillo (advertising).

Pictured here are, from left to right, Joe Coelho (produce warehouse), Carolyn McInerney, and Mary Coelho.

Pictured here are, from left to right, Helene Robert, Tita Baysa, Lori Cabreira-Barra (quality assurance), and Melanie Nable.

Pictured here are Donetta Gunderson-Jansen (left, marketing), and Martha Reyes (product promotions).

Pictured here are, from left to right, John Spohn (store manager), Bill Roth (electronic marketing), Vickey Oster, Ray Swain (buying), and Debbie Roth.

Pictured are Paul Knerr (pharmacy) and Dora Zavala (corporate brands).

Pictured here are, from left to right, (first row) Ruuda (Carriere) Pender and Norma (Kentner) Risher; (second row) Terry Grams (payroll), Rubina Merchant, Debra Bye, Ruby (Rivers) Douglas (human resources), Jenny (Miller) Hanna (vice president treasurer), Donna (Kaufman) Tyler (human resources), and Midge Young (human resources).

Pictured here are, from left to right, Audrey Caputo (space planning), Robert Kluger (real estate), Beverly Kluger (grocery buying), and Mike and Heather Princiotta.

Pictured here are, from left to right, Sarah Heck Griffin (advertising), Suzanne Dyer, Jo Ann Murdock, Leanne McKenzie, Chris Alvarez (corporate communications), Mary McAboy Del Santo, Sandra Calderon (corporate communications), Kris Tescher (electronic marketing), Mary Thompson (finance and planning), and Marcella Gelman (consumer affairs),

Pictured here are, from left to right, Mitchell Crawford (management information systems), Arif Merchant (planning), Bonnie Diener, Russ Doyle, Cel (Martinez) Avila, and John Weber (executive offices).

Pictured here are, from left to right, Dan and Barbara (Giovanni) Baisley, Evelyn Caruso (drugstore), John Caruso, LuAnn Johnson (deli-dairy buying), and Lynn Reyes-Trujillo.

Pictured here are the authors of this book and reunion committee chairs Mike Stark and Wendy Kennedy.

Consistent with our mission to preserve history on a local level, this book was printed in South Carolina on American-made paper and manufactured entirely in the United States. Products carrying the accredited Forest Stewardship Council (FSC) label are printed on 100 percent FSC-certified paper.

MADE IN THE USA